The Civil Rights Movement and Vietnam

1960–1976

SADDLEBACK
EDUCATIONAL PUBLISHING

Saddleback's *Graphic American History*

3 7548 00027 0913

ISBN-13: 978-1-59905-367-7
ISBN-10: 1-59905-367-5
eBook: 978-1-60291-695-1

Printed in Guangzhou, China
NOR/0313/CA21300172

17 16 15 14 13   4 5 6 7 8 9

When the 13th Amendment to the Constitution, making slavery illegal everywhere in the United States, was passed in the House of Representatives in 1865, there was wild cheering and great excitement.

For the slaves themselves, a new way of life began.

At a meeting of the American Anti-Slavery Society in New York, William Lloyd Garrison proposed disbanding.

It is an absurdity to maintain an anti-slavery society after slavery is killed.

But Wendell Phillips disagreed.

I fear you are too hopeful. To achieve civil equality before the law, for the black American a struggle still lies ahead.

The struggle did continue. Some of the greatest civil rights achievements have taken place since World War II.

In the 1936 Olympic Games in Berlin, Jesse Owens, a black American athlete, broke several world records.

Ralph Metcalf and Eddie Tolan also set records.

Adolph Hitler, the most bigoted racist leader of modern times, was furious. He left the stands rather than watch Owens and other African Americans receive their medals.

In World War II, more than a million African Americans fought in the armed forces against Hitler and the Nazis. Gradually, types of service and training were opened to them that had been closed to them in previous wars.

Integration in army ground troops began in 1945 when volunteer black infantrymen fought beside white soldiers in Germany.

Eighteen Liberty ships were named for African Americans.

Captain Hugh Mulzac, reporting to the SS *Booker T. Washington* to take command.

Yes, sir.

In the Merchant Marine, 24,000 African Americans served in mixed crews, some commanded by black officers.

Under Colonel Benjamin O. Davis Jr., the 332nd Fighter Group, all black, flew more than 3,000 missions in Europe.

They destroyed 300 enemy planes. Eighty-eight pilots, including Colonel Davis, received the Distinguished Flying Cross.

In 1950 in the Korean War, black and white soldiers fought together in integrated units, and Davis served as chief of staff of United States forces.

In 1946, President Truman set up the President's Committee on Civil Rights.

The preservation of civil liberties is the duty of every government—state, federal, and local.

But when state or local governments fail, the obligation falls back onto the federal establishment.

4

By executive order, Truman ended segregation in the armed forces and federal government. But his effort to push stronger civil rights laws through Congress were defeated by southern Democrats and conservative Republicans.

The next civil rights milestone came from the Supreme Court on May 17, 1954.

In the field of public education, the doctrine of "separate but equal" has no place. Separate educational facilities are inherently inequal!

George Hayes, Thurgood Marshall, and James Nabrit Jr., black lawyers who led the fight against school integration, congratulated each other.

Governor Byrnes of South Carolina gave a Southern reaction.

I am shocked. I urge all our people, white and colored, to exercise restraint and preserve order.

In 1956, campaigning for reelection, President Eisenhower made a speech at the Miami Airport.

Equality must be achieved finally in the hearts of men rather than in legislative halls.

6

Between 1954 and 1956, several hundred school districts throughout the country abandoned racially segregated classes.

On September 3, 1957, a court-approved desegration plan was to go into effect in Little Rock, Arkansas.

The NAACP doesn't like this plan—the admission of only a few black children to one senior high school.

But the night before, Governor Faubus made a surprise television address.

It's not enough of course, but at least it's a beginning.

It will not be possible to restore or to maintain order if forcible integration is carried out tomorrow.

I am therefore posting National Guardsmen outside Central High, to act not as segregationists or integrationists, but as soldiers.

A message came from the school board.

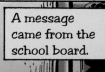

The school board will appeal to the federal judge that Governor Faubus has not used the troops to preserve law and order.

The next morning the federal judge handed down a ruling.

I will take the governor's word that the troops are neutral. I order the desegregation plan into effect forthwith!

On September 4, nine black children tried to exercise their legal right to go to Central High. The National Guard was there. So was a mob.

They're coming! Here they come!

Fifteen-year-old Elizabeth Ann Eckford walked quietly up to a school door.

A National Guardsman barred her way.

Go on home!

Alone, Elizabeth Ann walked back past the jeering, threatening crowd to the bus stop.

She's scared. She's just a little girl!

What are you doing, you loner?

By the next day, the FBI had agents at Little Rock investigating the situation. Governor Faubus spoke again.

I have wired the president to stop the unwarranted interference of federal agents!

That's telling 'em governor!

President Eisenhower made public his reply.

The only assurance I can give Governor Faubus is that the Federal Constitution will be upheld by me by every legal means at my command.

The violence and disorder continued. Finally, Eisenhower ordered 1,000 paratroopers to Little Rock and placed 10,000 members of the Arkansas National Guard on federal service to put down the mob. For the first time since Reconstruction, federal troops were sent into the South to protect African Americans.

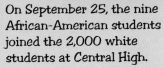

On September 25, the nine African-American students joined the 2,000 white students at Central High.

There was violence in the community as well as at the school. Homes of integration leaders were bombed.

Crosses were burned on their lawns.

Anti-integrationists kept violence alive in Little Rock for three years. But at last, Ernest Green became the first black graduate of an integrated Central High School.

By 1962 the formerly all-white high schools in Little Rock were desegregated. The battle for school integration in the South was not won—but at least it was successfully begun.

★ ★ ★ ★ ★ ★ ★ ★ ★ ★ ★ ★ ★ ★

The Civil War began in 1861, almost 100 years before the beginning of school integration. The 14th and 15th Amendments, passed at the end of the war, were virtually ineffective until the civil rights movement.

In 1955, in Montgomery, Alabama, the civil rights movement began only a few miles from what was the Confederacy's capital for the first few months of the Civil War.

There, on an evening in 1955, Mrs. Rosa Parks got on a bus tired from work.

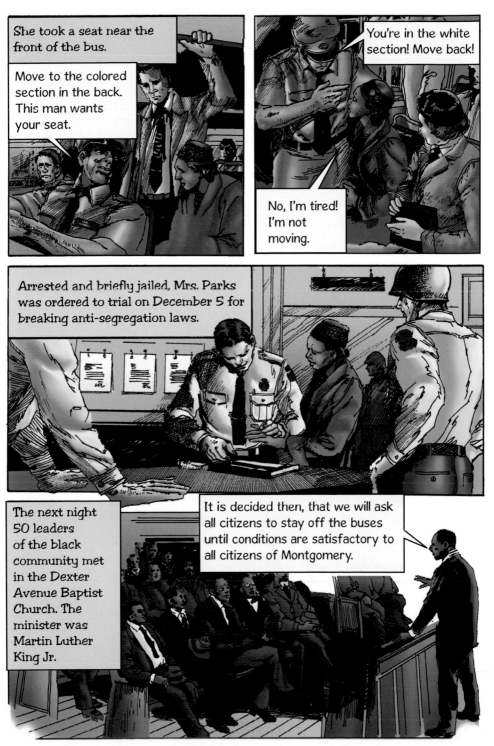

The Montgomery bus boycott was under way. Since 65% of the riders had been blacks, the buses on the streets were nearly empty.

Sure I'm tired, walking four miles home after working all day. But I won't take a bus!

There were frequent evening meetings. Again and again, African Americans listened to Martin Luther King Jr.

Our victory will not be for Montgomery alone. It will be a victory for justice, a victory for democracy. It is one of the greatest glories of America that we have the right to protest.

This is not a war between the white and the Negro ... this is bigger. If we are arrested every day, don't let anyone pull you so low as to hate them. We must use the weapon of love.

In November 1956, the Supreme Court issued its ruling.

This court unanimously confirms the order that bus segregation violates the Constitution.

Shortly before Christmas, the boycott ended.

You mean we just get on the bus and take the first seat we come to.

Inside, blacks and whites sat together.

Yes, sir, that's right!

I see that this is now the way it is going to be.

Frankly, I can't understand what all the fuss has been about.

A grandmother was interviewed by a reporter.

Jim Crow, he's more than 100 years old and real tired. We figure we've about put up long enough with tired things.

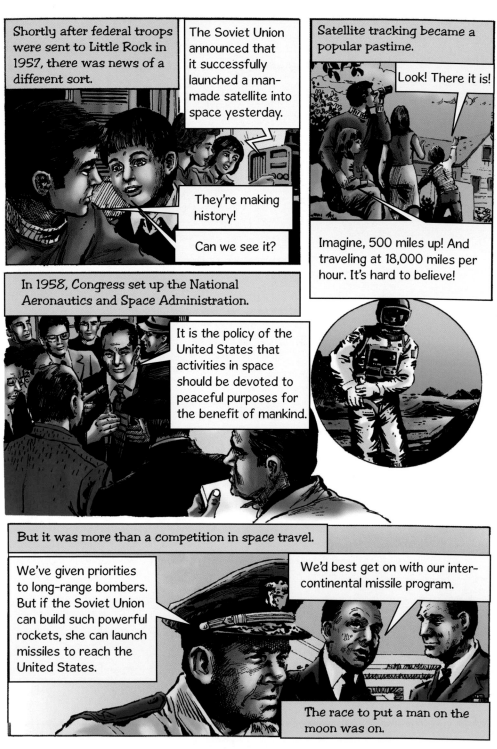

Shortly after federal troops were sent to Little Rock in 1957, there was news of a different sort.

The Soviet Union announced that it successfully launched a man-made satellite into space yesterday.

They're making history!

Can we see it?

Satellite tracking became a popular pastime.

Look! There it is!

Imagine, 500 miles up! And traveling at 18,000 miles per hour. It's hard to believe!

In 1958, Congress set up the National Aeronautics and Space Administration.

It is the policy of the United States that activities in space should be devoted to peaceful purposes for the benefit of mankind.

But it was more than a competition in space travel.

We've given priorities to long-range bombers. But if the Soviet Union can build such powerful rockets, she can launch missiles to reach the United States.

We'd best get on with our inter-continental missile program.

The race to put a man on the moon was on.

On April 12, 1961, there was another announcement on Moscow radio.

Russia has successfully launched a man into space. His name is Yuri Gagarin.

It's like science fiction.

On May 6, the Americans had their turn to rejoice. They could watch it on television.

Two ... one ... zero ... blast-off!

They listened to Alan Shepard's comment during his 15-minute flight.

All systems go. Everything OK. Coming in for a landing.

They could see for themselves as Shepard was welcomed aboard the recovery ship, that he was all right.

For several years, French forces in Indochina had been fighting a Communist rebel group, the Viet Minh. Under President Eisenhower, the United States policy of trying to prevent the forceful spread of Communism was continued. We aided the French with money, bombers, and other equipment, plus air force technicians to service the planes.

On May 7, 1954, after a siege of 50 days, the French base of Dien Bien Phu fell to the rebel forces.

In Geneva, on July 21, the French and Vietnamese signed an armistice.

In September, U.S. Secretary of State Dulles announced a new treaty.

The United States, Great Britain, France, Australia, New Zealand, Philippine Republic, Thailand, and Pakistan have formed the Southeast Asia Treaty Organization (SEATO), to oppose further Communist aggression in the area.

The governments of Laos and Cambodia were recognized by the Communists. Vietnam was divided into two parts: the Communist north and the Democratic south.

In Cuba, in 1959, rebels under the leadership of Fidel Castro overthrew the dictatorship of President Fulgencio Batista.

The United States quickly recognized the Castro government.

Batista was a dictator! The Cuban people had a hard time.

Castro promises to build a democracy and hold free elections.

But Castro postponed the elections. He executed hundreds of his enemies. And he became increasingly dependent upon the Soviet Union.

Many thousands of refugees fled from Cuba to Florida.

In 1960, Americans held a presidential election. The two candidates, Senator John F. Kennedy and Vice President Richard M. Nixon, met in a series of television debates.

No Roman Catholic had been elected president. Kennedy, a Catholic, spoke to the Houston Ministerial Association on September 12.

I believe in an America where the separation of church and state is absolute.

In a close election, Kennedy, great-grandson of Irish immigrants, became the first Catholic and the youngest man ever elected to the office of president.

Soon after his inauguration, Kennedy announced the formation of a Peace Corps to send Americans to help improve living conditions in underdeveloped countries.

It will not be easy. None will be paid a salary. They will live at the same level as the citizens of the country.

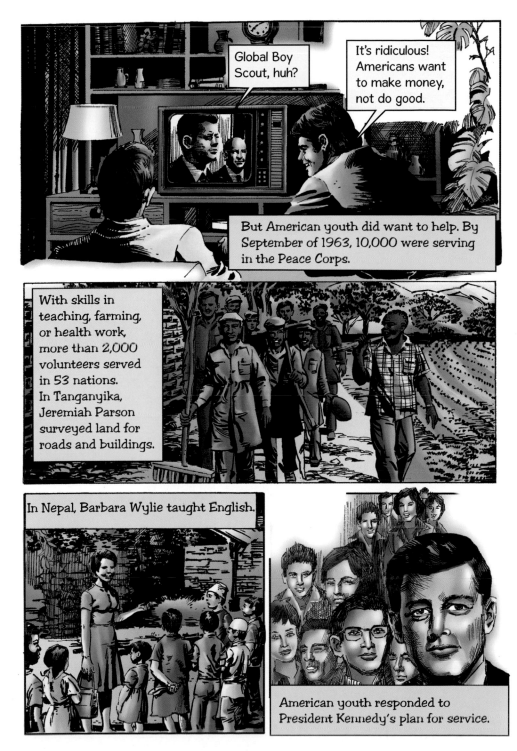

Global Boy Scout, huh?

It's ridiculous! Americans want to make money, not do good.

But American youth did want to help. By September of 1963, 10,000 were serving in the Peace Corps.

With skills in teaching, farming, or health work, more than 2,000 volunteers served in 53 nations. In Tanganyika, Jeremiah Parson surveyed land for roads and buildings.

In Nepal, Barbara Wylie taught English.

American youth responded to President Kennedy's plan for service.

Kennedy asked Congress to extend unemployment insurance, especially in areas like Appalachia where jobs had been scarce for a long time; to increase the minimum wage; for federal aid to education; more public housing; aid to farmers; and for medical insurance for people over 65.

In his campaign, he had committed himself to the explosive race-relations revolution.

Only a president willing to use all the resources of his office, can provide the leadership, the determination, and the direction to eliminate racial and religious discrimination from American society.

Much of this responsibility fell upon the attorney general, the president's brother, Robert Kennedy.

You'll be accused of favoritism if you appoint me attorney general.

Should I lose the best man for the job, just because he is my brother?

Robert Kennedy brought into the Justice Department a strong staff, including Burke Marshall.

I want you as my assistant in charge of the civil rights division.

There is a lot to be done.

In 1961, black students began a series of freedom rides to protest segregation in the South.

It's not just riding in the back of the bus. It's the separate waiting rooms, separate ticket windows, separate toilets—and all of them dirty!

And too bad if we get hungry, the lunch counters won't serve us!

Let's just go and sit in the white sections. No violence, just sit.

At bus stations, the rioters were met by angry mobs.

Busloads of people, both black and white, all pledged to non-violence rode into the South. Entering Alabama, one bus was stoned and burned.

The attorney general sent 500 federal marshals to Alabama to maintain order. The governor of Alabama objected.

Wire him that we do not need their help. We do not want their help, and we do not want them here in Alabama.

Kennedy replied.

Tell the governor that the United States government needs assurance by actions, not words, that its citizens will be safe in Alabama.

As a result of the opposition to the freedom riders, Kennedy obtained an order from the Interstate Commerce Commission outlawing segregation on all trains and buses and in terminals.

In January 1961, James Meredith, a young black Air Force veteran and a native of Mississippi, applied for admission to the University of Mississippi at Oxford.

Governor Ross Barnett announced that he would defy the federal law.

White Mississippians were outraged.

There's never been a black person at Ole Miss, and we'll see to it there will never be.

Represented by the NAACP, Meredith filed suit in court on the grounds that he had been turned down because of his race. After a long legal battle, a federal court ruled in Meredith's favor.

We will not surrender to the evil and illegal forces of tyranny.

24

In the late afternoon, Meredith arrived on campus with a group of federal marshals who escorted him to his dormitory.

Governor Barnett had given his word that the highway patrol could and would maintain order. But by sunset, a crowd began to gather.

Instead of interfering, the state troopers withdrew. Cars full of white men drove on to the campus.

For two hours the marshals stood quietly under attack, some bleeding from the bricks and bottles that were thrown. Then the crowd of 2,500 began to move in, and tear gas was fired.

Federal troops were called in. For 15 hours a full-scale riot raged, directed principally at federal marshals and newsmen. Snipers fired from the darkness. Two men were killed, hundreds wounded, including a third of the marshals. Cars and army trucks were burned.

Soon, 5,000 troops patrolled Oxford and the campus.

But Meredith was enrolled and attended classes, even though a small army was required for the victory.

It was a long, lonely time until his graduation in 1963. But a principle had been established.

Three weeks later, the president again spoke to the American people to tell them the Soviet Union, contrary to promises, was building offensive missile bases in Cuba.

The purpose of the bases can be none other than to provide a nuclear strike capability against the Western Hemisphere.

For two months, there had been reports of Russian ships landing technicians, planes, and missiles in Cuba.

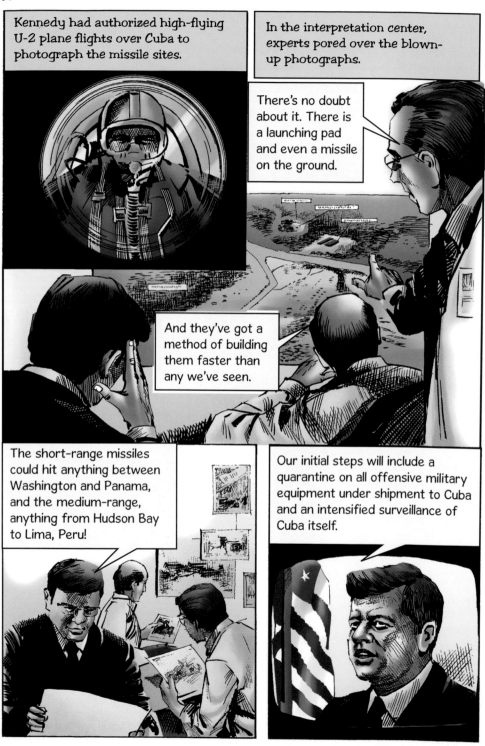

Kennedy had authorized high-flying U-2 plane flights over Cuba to photograph the missile sites.

In the interpretation center, experts pored over the blown-up photographs.

There's no doubt about it. There is a launching pad and even a missile on the ground.

And they've got a method of building them faster than any we've seen.

The short-range missiles could hit anything between Washington and Panama, and the medium-range, anything from Hudson Bay to Lima, Peru!

Our initial steps will include a quarantine on all offensive military equipment under shipment to Cuba and an intensified surveillance of Cuba itself.

It shall be the policy of this nation to regard any nuclear missile launched from Cuba against any nation in the Western Hemisphere as an attack by the Soviet Union on the United States requiring full retaliatory response on the Soviet Union.

What does it mean?

It means the Russians are setting up offensive missile bases 90 miles off of our coast!

Does it mean war?

If the Russians really meant war, I'd say yes. But it is just a threat. Kennedy has given them a chance to back down.

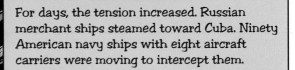

For days, the tension increased. Russian merchant ships steamed toward Cuba. Ninety American navy ships with eight aircraft carriers were moving to intercept them.

28

On June 19, 1963, Kennedy sent to Congress the most sweeping civil rights legislation in history. On August 28, 200,000 people, mostly black but many white, gathered peacefully in Washington to demonstrate their support.

In the afternoon, Dr. Martin Luther King Jr. addressed the people.

I have a dream ... that one day this nation will live out the true meaning of its creed ... all men are created equal ...

... that one day even the state of Mississippi ... will be transformed into an oasis of freedom and justice.

On November 22, 1963, President and Mrs. Kennedy flew to Dallas, Texas, where they were greeted by the Texas governor.

In a motorcade, they drove through cheering crowds toward downtown Dallas.

Suddenly, a sniper from a nearby building fired three shots, fatally wounding the president. The governor was injured. The entire world was stunned, grieved, almost unbelieving. A short time later, Lee Harvey Oswald, a one-time defector to the Soviet Union was arrested and accused of the crime.

On the presidential plane, as Mrs. Kennedy stood by, 90 minutes after the president's death, the vice president, Lyndon B. Johnson, was sworn in as the 36th president.

Two days later, in sight of television viewers across the nation, Oswald was shot and killed in the Dallas jail by Jack Ruby.

Later, a special presidential commission found no evidence of a conspiracy.

As the nation mourned, Johnson tried to pick up the pieces.

This is a sad time for all people. We have suffered a loss that cannot be weighed. I will do my best. That is all I can do. I ask your help, and God's.

People listened and thought the new president, Lyndon Baines Johnson, might do the job.

He's from Texas, the first southern president since the Civil War!

More than that, he's one of the most experienced politicians ever to become president. I think he'll do a fine job.

On June 19, 1964, Congress passed the strong civil rights bill that both Johnson and Kennedy had worked for.

It's a challenge to men of good will to transform the commands of our law into the custom of our land.

It is now the nation's task to conquer the barriers of poor education, poverty, and squalid housing, which are an inheritance of past injustice.

Johnson was declaring a war on poverty. But the United States was involved in a more destructive kind of war in Southeast Asia.

On August 2 in the Gulf of Tonkin, the U.S. destroyer *Maddox* was attacked by hostile North Vietnamese torpedo boats.

Johnson ordered retaliatory strikes on shore bases in North Vietnam.

The Senate approved.

Today, the Senate approved a resolution authorizing the president to take all necessary steps, including the use of the armed forces, to defend the free states in Southeast Asia.

So did the American people. In November, Johnson was overwhelmingly elected president in his own right.

With Johnson's victory, the Democrats won large majorities in Congress, enabling Johnson to enact much of his legislative program to build the "Great Society." This included the Economic Opportunity Act to train unemployed young people for jobs; federal aid to education; the Medicare bill; and additional civil rights acts.

A new cabinet post was created, the Department of Housing and Urban Development. Johnson introduced the new secretary, Robert Weaver.

There is no doubt the cities are in trouble, sir. Could you outline some of your plans?

In a poor African-American section of Los Angeles called Watts, violence erupted in the hot August of 1965.

Rioting, looting, and burning spread over a 13-square mile area and continued for four days. Twenty-one were killed, 600 hurt, 20,000 National Guard troops were required to restore order.

Martin Luther King Jr. preached nonviolence and love. Other African Americans, in their frustration, turned to radical groups.

In 1967, in Cleveland, Ohio, Carl Stokes was elected mayor in a close election, the first African-American mayor of a major U.S. city.

In July 1967, a riot broke out in Detroit in which more than 40 people were killed, blocks of buildings burned, thousands left homeless.

President Johnson spoke on television.

We must undertake an attack—mounted at every level—upon the conditions that breed despair and violence.

Close to Watts in Los Angeles was another poverty-stricken ghetto, a *barrio*, whose Mexican-American residents were beginning to speak out.

There are five million Mexican Americans in the United States. We are poorer, our housing is worse, our unemployment rate is higher, our educational level lower than any other group! What about us?

In California we outnumber the blacks by two to one, but where are the government programs to help us?

Man, if East L.A. ever blows, it will really blow!

In March 1968, the students of five high schools in the nation's largest Mexican-American community in Los Angeles, walked out in a mass demonstration.

VIVA LA RAZA

VIVA LA RAZA!

VIVA LA Revolucion

In response to the protests from many Mexican-American groups that their problems were being overlooked, a cabinet-level committee on Mexican-American affairs was established. Vicente T. Ximenes was appointed to hear problems and seek solutions.

The most widely recognized Mexican-American problem was that of the farm workers, with an average annual wage of $1,500 and dreadful living conditions. Organized by Cesar Chavez into the nonviolent United Farm Workers of America, they attracted national attention during the grape boycott and strike in 1965.

The most dramatic event was the 25 day march of the workers from Delano to Sacramento.

Starting with 75 men, the marchers swelled to a crowd of 4,000 for their arrival at the state capital on Easter Sunday.

Martin Luther King Jr. wired his good wishes to Chavez.

The fight for equality must be fought on many fronts— in the urban slums, in the sweat shops of factories, and fields. Our separate struggles are really one.

From Truman and Eisenhower, President Kennedy had inherited a commitment to prevent a Communist takeover in South Vietnam. It was a special kind of fighting.

A new type of soldier was trained to fight it—a special corps of guerrilla fighters, the Green Berets.

This is a new kind of war fought not by massive divisions but secretly by terror, ambush, and infiltration.

Truman sent 35 military advisers. Eisenhower sent 500 more. Still the Communists were winning, so Kennedy sent 15,000 troops.

After the Gulf of Tonkin Resolution by Congress authorizing him to take all necessary steps, Johnson sent more troops. By 1966, 375,000 Americans were fighting in Vietnam.

Your primary task is to train and strengthen the South Vietnamese forces; but you are authorized to fire at the enemy.

Many Americans were disturbed by this all-out war. Some young men burned their draft cards in protest.

In October 1967, 35,000 people protested the war in a march on Washington, stuffing the guns of the military police with flowers.

Senator Eugene McCarthy of Minnesota announced that he would run against Johnson in the Democratic presidential primaries as an anti-war candidate.

Soon Robert F. Kennedy, brother of the late president, made a similar announcement.

Then two events sent waves of sorrow, shock, outrage, and despair over the country.

APRIL 5

Dr. Martin Luther King Jr., who preached nonviolence and racial brotherhood, was fatally shot in Memphis last night by a sniper.

Oh my God, no!

The president, speaking from the White House, deplored the brutal slaying. He has set Sunday as a day of mourning for Dr. King.

From all over the country, black and white leaders gathered to attend Dr. King's funeral and to express sympathy to his family.

Two months later, on June 6, 1968, Robert Kennedy celebrated the winning of the California Democratic election primary.

Then shots rang out. Now it was Robert Kennedy, friend of the blacks, the Chicanos, of all the underprivileged young Americans, who fell to an assassin's bullet.

Robert Kennedy died on June 6, 1968. Dr. King's assassin, James Earl Ray, was later captured and sentenced. Sirhan Sirhan, the killer of Robert Kennedy received a similar prison sentence.

Once again, thousands gathered to mourn and to wonder what was happening to America.

The war protests increased. By 1968, about 10,000 young Americans had emigrated to Canada to escape the draft.

Thurgood Marshall was appointed by Johnson as the first African-American justice on the Supreme Court of the United States.

And Shirley Chisholm, a Democrat from New York, became the first African-American congresswoman.

My rise has been meteoric. I know I am a symbol.

On March 31, President Johnson spoke to Americans on television.

I am taking the first step to de-escalate the conflict. I have ordered our aircraft to make no attacks except immediately north of the demilitarized zone.

In November, in a close election, Richard Nixon was elected president.

That will be the great objective of this administration, to bring the American people together!

In his inauguration address, Nixon spoke of peace.

The greatest honor history can bestow is the title of peacemaker.

Both the American and the Russian space programs had been continuing. On July, 16, 1969, the American Apollo 11 mission blasted off for the moon.

It was 102 hours and 46 minutes later when Neil Armstrong, on a lunar module, detached from the spacecraft and radioed back to Earth.

Tranquility Base here. The *Eagle* has landed.

Then, as a worldwide audience estimated at 600 million people watched, men walk on another world. In New York, thousands watched the moonwalk on large screens set up in Central Park.

That's one small step for man, one giant leap for mankind.

Planting an American flag on the moon, Buzz Aldrin saluted it.

This certainly has to be the most historic telephone call ever made!

On October 15, 1969, all over America people gathered in a rally for peace.

But there were anti-protest protests.

And construction workers' demonstrations.

BOMB THE REDS

THERE'S NO GLORY LIKE OLD GLORY

WE LOVE AMERICA

NO SURRENDER

WE SUPPORT NIXON ON VIETNAM

In the spring of 1970, America seemed to be blowing apart: bombings, bomb threats, bomb factories, fires, student revolts, the takeover of college buildings. Then came the tragedy at Kent State University.

At Kent State in Ohio, National Guard troops fired into a crowd of demonstrating students. Four of the students were killed.

All over the country students went on strike. Four hundred colleges were closed, as students organized to bring pressure on Congress and the president.

Many spent their time collecting signatures for anti-war petitions.

By April 15, Nixon had withdrawn 115,000 troops from Vietnam. A welfare plan was before Congress. A revenue-sharing plan was in the works. Plans for environmental protection and control were in operation. And Henry Kissinger, the president's chief adviser on foreign affairs, made a secret visit to the People's Republic of China.

In July, newscasters reported the purpose of Kissinger's visit.

It has been announced that arrangements have been made for a personal meeting between President Nixon and Chinese Premier Chou En-lai.

It is probable that the president, accompanied by Mrs. Nixon, will visit the Republic of China sometime early next year.

Nixon visiting the head of Communist China! That really is news!

For nearly 25 years the United States had supported the Nationalist Chinese government of Chiang Kai-shek as the true government of China. The United States had opposed the admission to the United Nations of the People's Republic of China.

On October 25, 1971, on a tense rollcall vote in the General Assembly, the United States was defeated on an issue which would admit the Chinese Communists.

The Chinese Nationalists were expelled, and their delegates left the assembly, symbolizing the great change.

On the morning of February 21, 1972, the changes in world relationships were further dramatized when *Air Force One* touched down on a runway in China, bringing President Nixon for the first visit of an American president behind the Bamboo Curtain of Communist China.

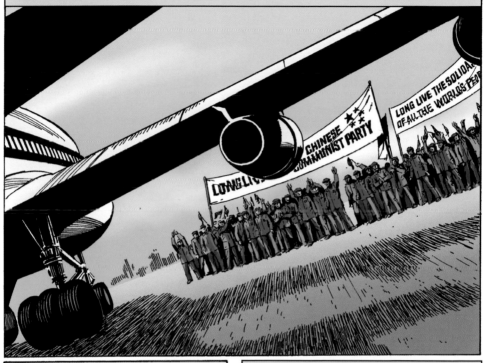

The American people watched on television as Nixon left the plane.

To Premier Chou En-lai, Nixon extended the hand of friendship, and Chou En-lai took it.

48

Later that day, Nixon was received by Chairman Mao Zedong.

Americans were treated to a Chinese travelogue as they watched the Nixons sightseeing.

They visited the Great Wall of China and its watchtowers, dating from 1368 C.E.

In a joint statement issued as result of the president's visit, he and Premier Chou emphasized that their talks showed the need for increased United States-Chinese relations. The United States recognized that Taiwan was part of China, and that the Taiwan question must be settled by the Chinese themselves, thus ending Washington's long support of Nationalist China.

In May 1972, Nixon visited the Soviet Union, where he and Soviet Communist Party leader Brezhnev signed two historic documents putting limits on the growth of strategic nuclear weapon supplies.

We want to be remembered by the fact that we made the world a more peaceful one for all people.

This is a great victory for all peaceloving people because security and peace is the common goal.

At 2 a.m. on June 17, the Washington police answered a call from the custodian of the Watergate Building. They arrested several men who had broken in to the offices of the Democratic National Headquarters.

Don't shoot. We give up!

One of the men arrested was James McCord, security chief of the Republican Committee to Re-elect the President (CREEP). In McCord's notebook was the telephone number of a White House employee.

President Nixon was re-elected by a landslide vote. On January 23, 1973, he appeared on television with an announcement.

We today have concluded an agreement to end the war and bring peace in Vietnam and Southeast Asia.

From Defense Secretary Laird on June 27, there was more news.

The armed forces henceforth will depend exclusively on volunteer soldiers. The use of the draft has ended.

But the Watergate break-in, the attempted cover-up, the leaks and rumor surrounding it, led to a Senate investigation of the integrity of the electoral process— in particular, of the 1972 presidential campaign.

The Ervin committee opened its hearing in the Senate caucus room on May 17, 1973. The first witness was Robert Odle, manager of CREEP's office staff.

Continuing through the summer, the hearings were followed on television by the nation.

On April 30, involved in the Watergate cover-up, Nixon's two top aides resigned. Nixon himself appeared on television to state that while he had not known about it, he accepted the responsibility.

Tonight I ask for your prayers, to help me in everything I do. God bless America, and God bless each and every one of you.

On October 11, Vice President Agnew appeared before Judge Walter E. Hoffman in a Baltimore courtroom and admitted to income tax invasion in 1967.

He also submitted his resignation as vice president effective immediately.

On August 29, Judge John J. Sirica ordered the controversial tape recordings of presidential conversations be submitted to him.

Ordered that respondent, Richard M. Nixon, is here by commanded to produce forthwith the subpoenaed documents.

The president refused to comply with the order.

On December 6, Gerald R. Ford was sworn in as the 40th vice president of the United States.

On Saturday evening, July 27, 1974, the 38 members of the House Judiciary Committee voted to recommend the impeachment of President Nixon.

The clerk will report the vote.

Twenty-seven members have voted *aye*, 11 members have voted no.

On August 8, President Nixon appeared on television again before the American people.

I shall resign the presidency effective at noon tomorrow.

The next day, Nixon said his goodbyes to members of his cabinet and staff.

Always remember others may hate you, but they don't win unless you hate them, and then you destroy yourself.

Then for the last time as president, he boarded the helicopter that carried him to the presidential jet, which had taken him all over the world. It was now to fly him home to California.

Once more, on August 9, Justice Burger administered an oath of office to Gerald Ford, this time as president of the United States.

Then Gerald Ford spoke to the nation.

I believe that truth is the glue that holds government together, not only our government, but civilization itself. That bond, though strained, is unbroken.

As we bind up the internal wounds of Watergate, more painful and more poisonous than those of foreign wars, let us restore the Golden Rule to the political process.

On September 9, President Ford issued a pardon to Nixon explaining his reasons.

Many months and perhaps more years will have to pass before Richard Nixon could obtain a fair trial by jury. During this long period of delay, ugly passions would again be aroused.

Many years ago, having finished his work at the Constitutional Convention, Benjamin Franklin was asked a question.

Mr. Franklin, what have you given us?

A republic, if you can keep it.

As President Kennedy forecast ...

No one expects that our life will be easy. History will not permit it. But we are still the keystone in the arch of freedom, and I think we will continue to do, as we have done in the past, our duty.